The Super BowL

All About Pro Football's
Biggest Event

by Hans Hetrick

SUPER BOWL

CAPSTONE PRESS

a capstone imprint

Sports Illustrated Kids Winner Takes All is published by Capstone Press,
1710 Roe Crest Drive, North Mankato, Minnesota 56003.
www.capstonepub.com

SI Kids is a trademark of Time Inc. Used with permission.

Library of Congress Cataloging-in-Publication Data
Hetrick, Hans, 1973–
    The Super Bowl : all about pro football's biggest event / by Hans Hetrick.
    p. cm.—(Edge books)
    Includes bibliographical references and index.
    Summary: "Describes the NFL's Super Bowl championship, including some of the
greatest teams, players, and moments from Super Bowl history"—Provided by publisher.
    ISBN 978-1-4296-6573-5 (library binding)
    ISBN 978-1-4296-9442-1 (paperback)
    1. Super Bowl—History—Juvenile literature. I. Title.
GV956.2.S8H48 2013
796.332'648—dc23   2011048857

Editorial Credits

Aaron Sautter, editor; Kazuko Collins, designer; Eric Gohl, media researcher;
    Laura Manthe, production specialist

Photo Credits

Getty Images: Dave Cross, 29, Focus on Sport, 20, Fotosports International,
25, Sports Imagery/Herb Scharfman, 16; Newscom: UPI Photo Service/
Bruce Gordon, 19, Zuma Press/Tony Tomsic, 10, 11, 27; Sports Illustrated: Al
Tielemans, 5, 9, Andy Hayt, 13, 26, Bill Frakes, cover (background), Bob Rosato,
cover (right), Damian Strohmeyer, 18 (front), 21, Heinz Kluetmeier, cover (left),
15, Hy Peskin, 7, John Biever, 2–3, 8, 23, John Iacono, 14, Peter Read Miller,
cover (middle), Robert Beck, 4, Simon Bruty, 22 (front), Walter Iooss Jr., 12

Design Elements

Shutterstock: MaxyM, Redshinestudio, rendergold

Records listed in this book are current as of
the 2011 season.

Printed in the United States of America in Stevens Point, Wisconsin.
042012   006678WZF12

· TABLE OF CONTENTS ·

Football's Biggest Stage

On February 5, 2012, the New York Giants were trailing 17-15 to the New England Patriots. Giants quarterback Eli Manning had one more chance to lead his team to a National Football League (NFL) championship. The Giants were 88 yards from the **end zone**. Less than four minutes remained in the game. But it wasn't a normal game. It was Super Bowl XLVI, the biggest game of the year.

Mario Manningham

end zone—the area between the goal line and the end line at either end of a football field

This was no ordinary Super Bowl. The Patriots and Giants had already faced each other four years earlier in Super Bowl XLII. New England had not lost a game that season. Few people thought the Giants could win. But Manning led the team to an amazing last-minute score to beat the Patriots 17-14 and win the title.

Now the two teams faced each other again. And once more, the Giants needed Manning to lead them to a last-minute win. On the first play of the drive, Manning threw a perfect pass between two Patriots defenders. Wide receiver Mario Manningham reached out to haul in the ball. When he came down, his feet barely touched down inbounds. The amazing 38-yard catch jump-started the Giants offense. Several plays later, they scored a touchdown to take the lead 21-17.

The Patriots had one last chance to win the game. But on the final play, Tom Brady's Hail Mary pass fell incomplete in the end zone. The Giants were Super Bowl champions again. Manning's performance earned him the Super Bowl Most Valuable Player (MVP) award.

Eli Manning

THE BIG SHOW

In 2012 more than 111 million Americans watched Super Bowl XLVI. It was the most watched program in the history of American television.

A Merger Marks the Beginning

The Super Bowl is the most popular sporting event in America. The Super Bowl resulted from the merger of the NFL and the American Football League (AFL). Formed in 1920, the NFL was the older, more established league. The AFL started in 1960 and featured a more exciting style of football. While the NFL emphasized the running game, AFL teams ran trick plays and threw more passes.

The AFL quickly became popular enough to rival the NFL. Instead of competing against the AFL, the NFL decided to become partners in 1966. The two leagues agreed to play a championship game each year, which they called the AFL-NFL World Championship. It was officially called the Super Bowl beginning in 1969.

In Super Bowls I, II, and III, the AFL champion faced the NFL champion for the title. The two leagues completed a merger in 1970. The new NFL included 28 teams and two new conferences. Most teams from the NFL became the National Football Conference (NFC). However, three NFL teams joined with the AFL to form the American Football Conference (AFC).

BALL   AT BAT   VISITORS   H   E
STRIKE   OUT INN. CLEVELAND   H   E

Before merging with the AFL, the NFL was split into two conferences.
Each year the conference champions played in the NFL Championship
Game. In 1954 the Cleveland Browns beat the Detroit Lions 56-10.

The road to the Super Bowl is long and demanding. Each NFL team plays a 16-game regular season. At the end of the season, the top six teams from the NFC and the AFC earn a spot in the NFL playoffs.

Green Bay Packers linebacker Diyral Briggs

The playoff teams include four division champions and two **wild card** teams from each conference. The top two division champions earn a **bye**. The other two division champions play the wild card teams in the first round of playoff games. The winners advance to the divisional playoffs. The divisional winners then play in the AFC and NFC title games. The conference champions face each other in the Super Bowl to play for the NFL championship title.

Pittsburgh Steelers tackle Marvel Smith

wild card—a team that advances to the playoffs without winning its division

bye—when a team has played well enough to automatically advance to the second round of the playoffs

Glorious Dynasties

Since the first Super Bowl, a few teams have outshined the others. These legendary teams are known as **dynasties**. The following teams possessed a quality that set them apart. They always found a way to win the title on football's biggest stage.

1960s – Green Bay Packers

The Green Bay Packers became the first dynasty of the Super Bowl age. The Packers were already a powerful team before winning Super Bowl I. Head coach Vince Lombardi and his Packers had already claimed three NFL championships earlier in the 1960s.

THE LOMBARDI TROPHY

The winner of the Super Bowl receives the Vince Lombardi Trophy. The trophy is named for the head coach of the first Super Bowl champions, the Green Bay Packers.

Vince Lombardi

dynasty—a team that wins multiple championships over a period of several years

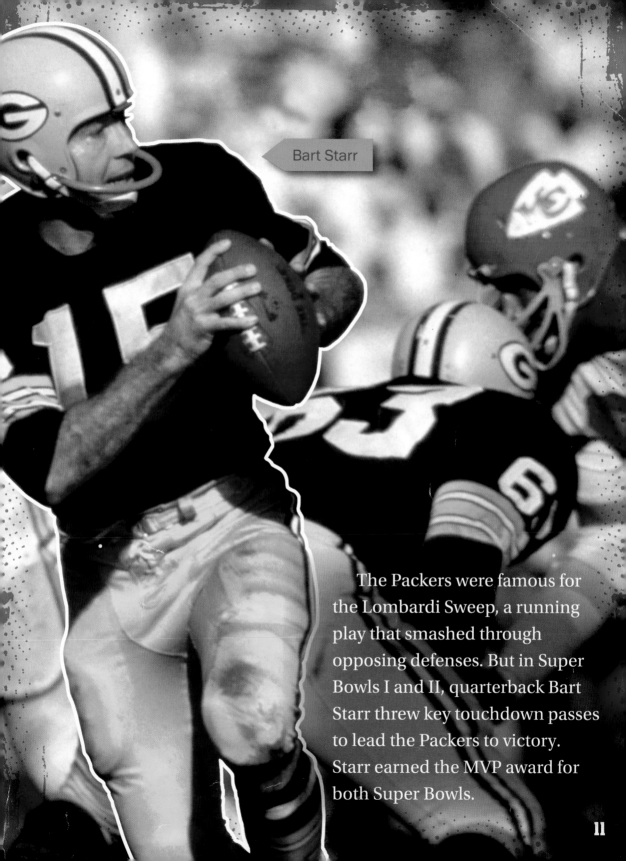

Bart Starr

The Packers were famous for the Lombardi Sweep, a running play that smashed through opposing defenses. But in Super Bowls I and II, quarterback Bart Starr threw key touchdown passes to lead the Packers to victory. Starr earned the MVP award for both Super Bowls.

The Pittsburgh Steelers struggled for nearly 40 years. Between 1933 and 1971, the Steelers made the playoffs only once. But in 1969 new head coach Chuck Noll began building one of the greatest teams the NFL has ever seen. In 1975 the Steelers beat the Minnesota Vikings 16-6 to win Super Bowl IX and their first title. The Steelers won another three Super Bowls in the next five years. Nine players from the 1970s Steelers teams are now in the Pro Football Hall of Fame.

Pittsburgh Steelers running back Franco Harris

1980s – San Francisco 49ers

The San Francisco 49ers were the team to beat in the 1980s. From 1981 to 1989, San Francisco won four Super Bowl titles. The 49ers' offense worked like a finely tuned machine. Receiver Jerry Rice sliced through opposing defenses with razor-sharp pass routes. Quarterback Joe Montana zipped passes into his receivers' hands with pinpoint accuracy. The 49ers' offense was the creation of head coach Bill Walsh. Walsh's offense, known as the West Coast offense, is still used by many NFL teams today.

Joe Montana

· MOST SUPER BOWL MVPs ·

JOE MONTANA	SAN FRANCISCO 49ERS	3
BART STARR	GREEN BAY PACKERS	2
ELI MANNING	NEW YORK GIANTS	2
TERRY BRADSHAW	PITTSBURGH STEELERS	2
TOM BRADY	NEW ENGLAND PATRIOTS	2

1990s – Dallas Cowboys

In 1989 the Cowboys finished with a disappointing 1–15 record. To improve the team, coach Jimmy Johnson made a blockbuster deal with the Minnesota Vikings. The Vikings got star running back Herschel Walker and four draft picks. The Cowboys received five veteran players and eight draft picks. Over the next few years, Dallas used those picks to help rebuild the team. In 1992 the Cowboys ran up a 13–3 regular season record on their way to the Super Bowl. With star players like quarterback Troy Aikman and running back Emmitt Smith, Dallas cruised to three Super Bowl titles from 1993 to 1996.

Troy Aikman

• MOST SUPER BOWL APPEARANCES •

DALLAS COWBOYS	8
PITTSBURGH STEELERS	8
NEW ENGLAND PATRIOTS	7
DENVER BRONCOS	6

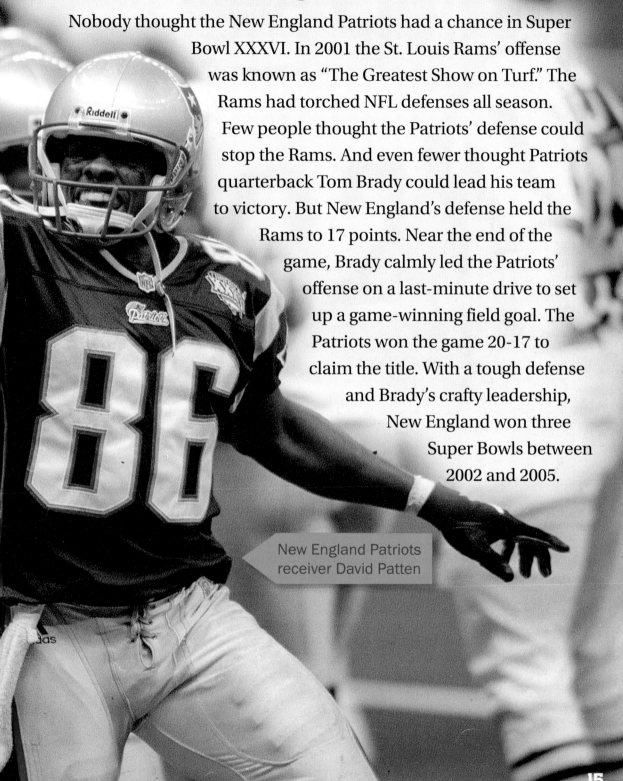

2000s – New England Patriots

Nobody thought the New England Patriots had a chance in Super Bowl XXXVI. In 2001 the St. Louis Rams' offense was known as "The Greatest Show on Turf." The Rams had torched NFL defenses all season. Few people thought the Patriots' defense could stop the Rams. And even fewer thought Patriots quarterback Tom Brady could lead his team to victory. But New England's defense held the Rams to 17 points. Near the end of the game, Brady calmly led the Patriots' offense on a last-minute drive to set up a game-winning field goal. The Patriots won the game 20-17 to claim the title. With a tough defense and Brady's crafty leadership, New England won three Super Bowls between 2002 and 2005.

New England Patriots receiver David Patten

Gridiron Heroes

Joe Namath

Sometimes one team jumps ahead and cruises to a big win. But when teams win the big game too easily, it's usually considered a dull game. However, teams often match each other play for play. There have been many exciting Super Bowls that football fans will never forget.

The Guarantee

Super Bowl III: New York Jets vs. Baltimore Colts

In the early Super Bowls, the NFL and the AFL were bitter rivals. Many fans believed the NFL teams were better. The AFL hadn't proved they could compete in the Super Bowl. In Super Bowls I and II, the Green Bay Packers had no problem defeating the AFL champions.

In 1969 the Baltimore Colts were expected to keep the NFL on top in Super Bowl III. But New York Jets quarterback Joe Namath had something different in mind. A few days before the game, "Broadway Joe" publicly guaranteed a Jets victory. To everyone's surprise, the Jets came through on Namath's guarantee and won 16-7. The AFL had proved it was a worthy opponent for the mighty NFL.

SUPER BALL AND THE SUPER BOWL

Lamar Hunt, owner of the Kansas City Chiefs, thought of the name for the NFL title game. His children loved playing with Super Balls. He jokingly called the title game the Super Bowl while thinking of the bouncy toy balls. The name became popular and was officially recognized by the league in 1969.

The Tackle

Super Bowl XXXIV: St. Louis Rams vs. Tennessee Titans

In 2000 the St. Louis Rams were in complete control of Super Bowl XXXIV. But late in the third quarter, the Tennessee Titans offense woke up. They scored 16 straight points to tie the game. Late in the fourth quarter, the Rams retook the lead when quarterback Kurt Warner threw a 73-yard touchdown pass to receiver Isaac Bruce. The Titans had less than two minutes to score a touchdown.

Isaac Bruce

THE TRAVELING FOOTBALL GAME

The Super Bowl is played at a different location each year. The NFL chooses a city to host the Super Bowl three to five years in advance.

Titans quarterback Steve McNair quickly moved his team to the Rams' 10-yard line. With only six seconds to go, the Titans called their final timeout. They had one last chance at a touchdown. McNair threw the ball to receiver Kevin Dyson, who raced for the end zone. But Rams linebacker Mike Jones was ready. He swept in and wrapped up Dyson's legs. Dyson dove for the goal line, but Jones held on tight. Dyson fell just inches from the end zone as time ran out. The Rams won the game 23-16. The final play of Super Bowl XXXIV became known as "The Tackle" and is considered one of the greatest moments in NFL history.

Kevin Dyson

The Helmet Catch

Super Bowl XLII: New York Giants vs. New England Patriots

The 2007 New England Patriots steamrolled into Super Bowl XLII with a record-setting 18–0 season. The Patriots offense seemed unstoppable. They had scored an NFL record 589 points. Quarterback Tom Brady had thrown a record 50 touchdown passes. Receiver Randy Moss had set an NFL record with 23 touchdown catches.

The New York Giants were big underdogs before the game. But they had a great defensive line. In the Super Bowl, the Giants' defense constantly **blitzed** Brady. He had to keep dodging the Giants' big defensive players and couldn't pile up points.

THE ONLY UNDEFEATED TEAM

The 1972 Miami Dolphins are the only team to finish an NFL season, including the playoffs, with a perfect record. If the 2007 Patriots had won the Super Bowl, they would have been the second team to achieve that rare feat. However, the Patriots are the only team to finish with a perfect regular-season record in a 16-game schedule. When the 1972 Dolphins had their perfect season, NFL teams played a 14-game schedule.

Miami Dolphins running back Larry Csonka

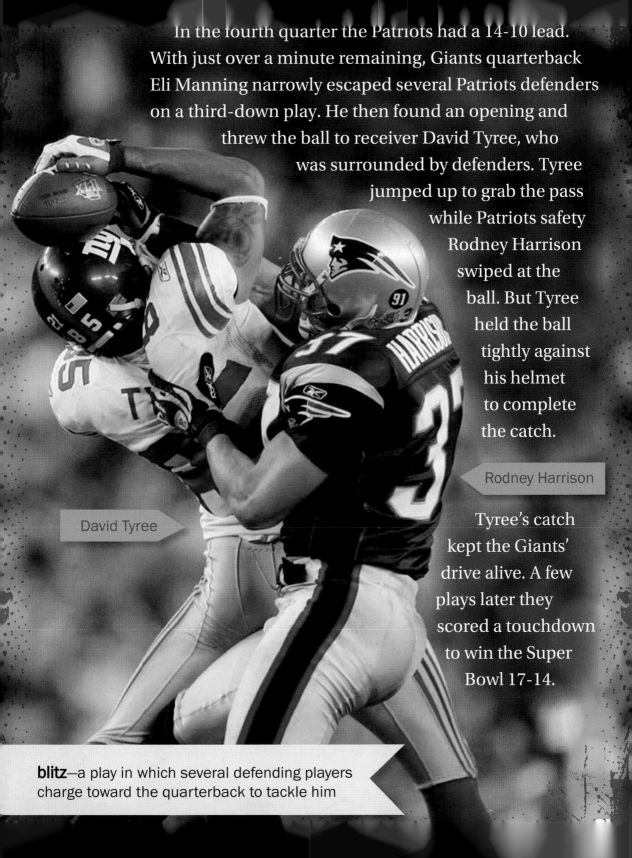

In the fourth quarter the Patriots had a 14-10 lead. With just over a minute remaining, Giants quarterback Eli Manning narrowly escaped several Patriots defenders on a third-down play. He then found an opening and threw the ball to receiver David Tyree, who was surrounded by defenders. Tyree jumped up to grab the pass while Patriots safety Rodney Harrison swiped at the ball. But Tyree held the ball tightly against his helmet to complete the catch.

Rodney Harrison

David Tyree

Tyree's catch kept the Giants' drive alive. A few plays later they scored a touchdown to win the Super Bowl 17-14.

blitz—a play in which several defending players charge toward the quarterback to tackle him

Both Feet Down

Super Bowl XLIII: Pittsburgh Steelers vs. Arizona Cardinals

In 2009 the Arizona Cardinals trailed the Pittsburgh Steelers 20-7 late in Super Bowl XLIII. But the Cardinals made a furious comeback. Quarterback Kurt Warner and receiver Larry Fitzgerald hooked up to quickly score two touchdowns. Arizona's defense added a **safety** to give the Cardinals a 23-20 lead.

With less than three minutes to go, the Steelers got the ball back. They were 78 yards from the end zone. Steelers quarterback Ben Roethlisberger rallied his team. He moved the Steelers offense to the Cardinals' six-yard line in only two minutes.

Kurt Warner

safety—when a player is tackled behind his own goal line; the defensive team is awarded two points and the ball

With less than a minute to go, Roethlisberger dropped back to pass. He slipped a tackle and threw the ball to the back of the end zone. The pass dropped behind three Cardinals defenders and into the hands of Steelers receiver Santonio Holmes. Holmes stretched out as far as possible to make the catch. But the officials weren't sure his feet were inbounds. Replays showed the very tips of his shoes scraped the grass in the end zone. The referees ruled the catch a touchdown, and the Steelers celebrated their incredible last-minute 27-23 Super Bowl victory.

Santonio Holmes

Wild and Surprising Moments

The Super Bowl can be incredibly unpredictable. Footballs can take crazy bounces and produce unexpected results. And players can surprise us with amazing performances. These wild moments are part of the reason so many fans love watching the big game.

Timmy Smith

Few people knew who Timmy Smith was before Super Bowl XXII. Smith was a rookie running back for the Washington Redskins. During the regular season, Smith had gained only 126 yards. But in 1988 he would run for more yards in the Super Bowl than he did the entire season. Smith busted through the Denver Broncos defense for 204 yards and two touchdowns. Smith's surprising performance led the Redskins to crush the Broncos 42-10.

People didn't see much of Timmy Smith after the Super Bowl. He retired after only three seasons with a total of 944 rushing yards. But Smith's record still stands as the most rushing yards gained by a single player in a Super Bowl.

CHAPTER 4

Timmy Smith

• MOST SUPER BOWL LOSSES •

BUFFALO BILLS	4
DENVER BRONCOS	4
MINNESOTA VIKINGS	4
NEW ENGLAND PATRIOTS	4

Garo's Goof

The mighty 1972 Miami Dolphins defense nearly **shut out** the Washington Redskins in Super Bowl VII.

But it wasn't meant to be. In the fourth quarter, the Dolphins were about to take a 17-0 lead. But the Redskins were ready as kicker Garo Yepremian lined up for his 42-yard field goal attempt. The Redskins blocked the kick, but the ball bounced right back to Yepremian.

THE SUPER BOWL SHUFFLE

The 1985 Chicago Bears didn't sing very well, but they were a confident team. Two months before the big game, the Bears recorded a song called "The Super Bowl Shuffle." Their confidence paid off. The Bears defeated the New England Patriots 46-10 in Super Bowl XX.

Otis Wilson (55) and William "The Refrigerator" Perry (72)

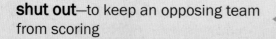

shut out—to keep an opposing team from scoring

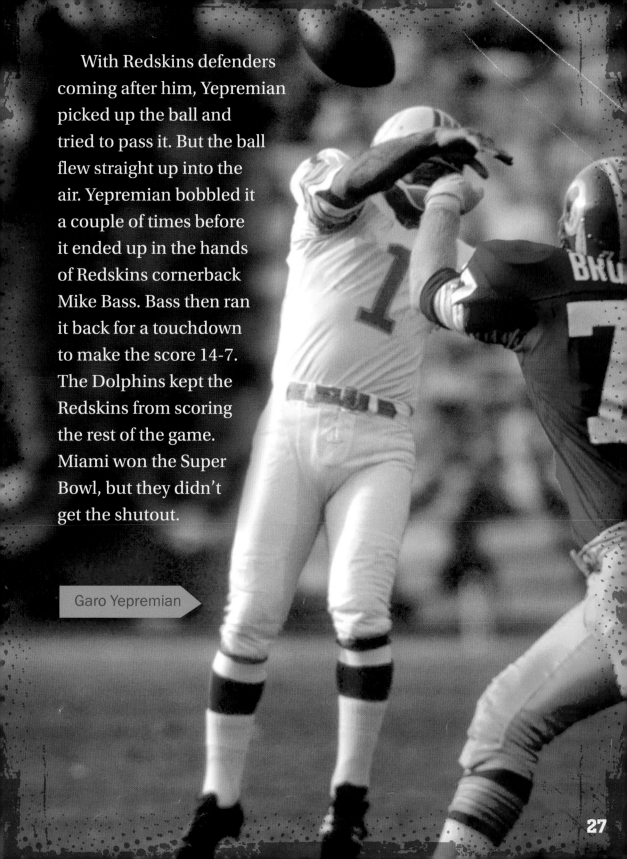

With Redskins defenders coming after him, Yepremian picked up the ball and tried to pass it. But the ball flew straight up into the air. Yepremian bobbled it a couple of times before it ended up in the hands of Redskins cornerback Mike Bass. Bass then ran it back for a touchdown to make the score 14-7. The Dolphins kept the Redskins from scoring the rest of the game. Miami won the Super Bowl, but they didn't get the shutout.

Garo Yepremian

Lett's Fumble

Leon Lett

In 1993 nothing seemed to go right for the Buffalo Bills in Super Bowl XXVII. The team was already getting beaten badly by the Dallas Cowboys. Then in the fourth quarter, Bills quarterback Frank Reich got hit and lost the ball. Dallas Cowboys defensive lineman Leon Lett picked it up and ran for the end zone.

But Lett started celebrating too early. He reached the ball out with one hand before crossing the goal line. Lett didn't see Bills wide receiver Don Beebe speeding up behind him. Beebe knocked the ball out of Lett's hand and through the end zone for a **touchback**. The Bills got the ball back, but they couldn't get back into the game. The Cowboys clobbered the Bills 52-17. Although his team won the title, Lett is still remembered more for his famous fumble.

touchback—when a football has been ruled dead behind a team's own goal line

Don Beebe

THE UNEXPECTED MVP

The MVP of Super Bowl V played for the losing team. Super Bowl V was an ugly game. The Dallas Cowboys and the Baltimore Colts combined for 10 turnovers. The Colts took home the trophy after winning the game 16-13. But it was Cowboys linebacker Chuck Howley who took home the MVP award. Howley earned the award for intercepting two of Colts quarterback Johnny Unitas' passes. Howley also recovered a fumble in the game.

GLOSSARY

blitz (BLITS)—a play in which several defending players charge toward the quarterback to tackle him

bye (BYE)—when a team has played well enough to automatically advance to the second round of the playoffs

dynasty (DYE-nuh-stee)—a team that wins multiple championships over a period of several years

end zone (END ZOHN)—the area between the goal line and the end line at either end of a football field

Hail Mary (HAYL MAY-ree)—a play where the quarterback throws the ball deep toward the end zone in the hope that one of the team's receivers will catch it

safety (SAYF-tee)—when a player is tackled behind his own goal line; the defensive team is awarded two points and the ball

shut out (SHUHT OUT)—to keep an opposing team from scoring

touchback (TUCH-bak)—when a football has been ruled dead behind a team's own goal line

turnover (TURN-oh-vur)—when a team loses possession of the ball

wild card (WILD CARD)—a team that advances to the playoffs without winning its division

READ MORE

Buckley, James. *Super Bowl Fireworks!* New York: Scholastic, 2009.

Frederick, Shane. *The Ultimate Guide to Pro Football Teams.* Ultimate Pro Guides. Mankato, Minn.: Capstone Press, 2010.

Gigliotti, Jim. *Super Bowl Super Teams.* New York: Scholastic, 2010.

INTERNET SITES

FactHound offers a safe, fun way to find Internet sites related to this book. All of the sites on FactHound have been researched by our staff.

Here's all you do:

Visit *www.facthound.com*

Type in this code: 9781429665735

INDEX